b sides

b sides

poems

Erin Wescott

for myself alone

INTRO

In 2020, I wrote hundreds of lyrics for a collective songwriting project online. As the pandemic stretched to multiple lockdowns, I began restacking those short lyrics to create the poems in this book. Line by line, random words and sentences came together to form sound in the silence.

This is what I heard in the empty in-between.

-halls like caverns empty-
-music no one hears-
-the aching stillness of another daybreak-
-footsteps quicken-
-ice breaking underfoot-
-punctuating-
-the wet darkness-
-all this waiting-
-a paradise of emptiness-
-we were never really here-

-rendered speechless-
-blowing all my lines-
-groping toward something-
-unscripted-
-perpetually mortified-
-the purest panic-
-tales of tenderness-
-bungled badly-
-caught between pages-
-listless with longing-

-in the shadow of helicon-
-ink bleeding on the page-
-a pyrrhic victory-
-dead end street-
-the hero never came-
-written through me-
-monuments of arrogance-
-on an empty stage-

-boomerang love-
-here and gone again-
-like a quantum doctor's cat-
-diving off your pedestal-
-when everything implodes-
-amplitude-
-too humble for humility-
-a primal wail-
-dying to be known-

-the sweetness of summer-
-dozing on the lawn-
-paws on patio-
-rattled lids-
-picnic pandemonium-
-panic in the park-

-hijacked hourglass-
-wrong side out-
-infinite hours-
-shaken to the core-
-the thief of time-
-shouting out the secret-
-we never had control anyway-

-a pyroclastic burst-
-fast and fevered-
-deepening to night-
-the final chord-
-passion in the pathos-
-stones in shadow-
-guard you while you sleep-

-stifled summer-
-paradise in ashes-
-in captivity, we fed upon each other-
-no outlet-
-starved for laughter-

-poisoned honey-
-lipstick labyrinth-
-this love like fighting crime-
-twisted metal-
-sheets tangled into morning-
-somewhere between us-
-the well ran dry-

-washed out-
-rain rattles on the roof-
-an autumn echo-
-carried on the wind-
-beneath my fingers-
-warming in your hand-
-hearts that keep good time-

-this love-
-taken on faith-
-met with kindness-
-drained of all my doubt-
-a thousand footsteps further-
-i'll meet you at the gate-

-the longest sentence-
-walking without you-
-patience-
-penitence-
-in aeternum-
-finding purchase-
-on my knees-

-tiny memories-
-taken from me-
-the scent of you-
-lost in time-
-driven beyond-
-breaking strain-
-awake alone-
-howling out your name-

-the fort in the woods-
-this will be our kingdom-
-startled laughter-
-tangled pathways-
-off and running-
-on a dare-
-crashing headlong into you-
-dizzy with forever-
-like falling from a star-

-the wind in your hair-
-the tide ran from us-
-with a whisper-
-skipping stones-
-happiness is born of this-

-a circus in my arms-
-kaleidoscopic blur-
-heightened need-
-beating in my chest-
-racing forward-
-called by another's name-
-midsummer madness-
-like cardiac arrest-

-the pause before the kiss-
-no escape from gravity-
-the end of the beginning-
-the earth is spinning me-

-twisting echoes of quiet churches-
-shadows touching shadows-
-at the edge of the abyss-
-devotion-
-demolition-
-exhaling more than exaltation-
-careless words-
-like gravity-
-faithless-

-watch over one another-
-facades are falling now-
-the strength we held within us-
-throwing down the stones-
-the shattering of silence-
-collective sorrow-
-we grow from the ashes-
-toes planted in the dirt-

-the moments blur-
-fraying at the edges-
-laurels in her hair-
-remembered bliss-
-old victories-
-in black and white-
-doe-eyed youth-
-lost and haunted-
-behind the mask of years-

-shades of autumn-
-chapel light-
-stolen afternoons-
-sliding into sunset-
-tender longing-
-yielding to a word-

-quiet hands-
-the damp of evening-
-leaning into you-
-my heartbeat in your veins-
-fireworks in the rain-

-the past few days-
-walking alongside-
-interlacing fingers-
-neither here, nor there-
-this is the present-
-the gifted moment-
-to be known, as myself-

-triumphant noise-
-passion turns to laughter-
-blanket forts-
-pleasure most mundane-
-gentle hands lifted-
-stealing all my shirts-
-warmed to the core-
-hidden from the world-

-barefoot in the snow-
-we danced on air-
-pent up laughter-
-flailing blindly-
-we cannot be contained-

-gulls call out your name-
-caught between two planes of blue-
-spinning outward-
-unmoored-
-neither east nor west, but home-

-waymarked-
-the path winds upward-
-my northern star-
-home fire's light-
-i find you everywhere-

-quantum entanglement-
-this polarity-
-light that answers light-
-truth like an arrow-
-for a moment in time-
-no difference only distance-

-blackholes dance-
-in lush embrace-
-the constant-
-calming clamor-
-like waves on water-
-beyond the laws of time and space-

-deep sea diver-
-you came unbidden-
-work of art-
-stillness of the deep-
-the measure of your worth-
-found in loss-
-your beauty lies in truth-
-stronger than fear-

-like a midnight swim-
-out to the breakers-
-phosphorescence-
-light upon water-
-a stolen sea of stars-
-i'll paint you in their light-

-the forest breathes-
-sweet forgotten magic-
-mystic circles-
-slender birches-
-a pure surrender-
-rising like the mist-

-don't promise me the world-
-for it's already mine-
-a misdirected atlas-
-weightless-
-i pulled down the moon-

0:34

-captured infinite-
-water in your palm-
-all i am-
-framed with fingers-
-so aching ordinary-
-a lifetime, still unknown-

-my best wish for you-
-the far horizon-
-fabled graces-
-quiet burning-
-perfect flow-
-dawn in the distance-
-calling you home-
-crowned in laurels-
-lofted wings-
-uncommon things-

-barbed words-
-cracking knuckles-
-last one chosen-
-crushed by doubt-
-you don't get to tell me i'm broken-

-love in fiction-
-can you read me-
-the answer in your silence-
-the writing on my wall-

-a tuneless dancer-
-radiating grace-
-stepping from the cliff-
-ascending joy-
-you bite your lip-
-in all your frailty-
-afraid to fall-
-you can wear my wings-

-my captured springtime-
-awake in quiet ruins-
-a glimpse of the garden-
-leveled by the storm-
-restless frisson-
-waiting like a metronome-
-caught and cloistered-
-alive beneath the stone-

0:40

-future perfect, present tense-
-i walked free-
-looking half-wrecked-
-no laurels, only thorns-

[BONUS]

bring the fire

every day
i stand half frozen
seeking warmth from my reflection
in the doorway of a furnace
that's been chained against the fire

put out by the sudden silence
voices smothered every way
though we'd kindle in a moment
if we heard the call to burn

ashen stillness on the pavement
where the rumble yet remains
of black boxes tumbling in
like coals to feed the flame

the dates out front keep changing
but the sound check stays the same
we are test test tested
unignited
every day

During lockdown, I walked past the local music hall every day. I wrote this about all the sidelined crews and everyone who works behind the scenes to make sure the shows go on. Thanks for bringing back the fire.

Erin Wescott is a librarian, writer, and accidental poet. Her writing has appeared on Vocal and in *Bramble* magazine.

She weathered the pandemic in Toronto, but has since returned home to Wisconsin.

Made in the USA
Monee, IL
05 June 2023

35052301R00036